If the outside world could be made aware of the inner commitments by which we are guided, it would understand our motivations better and be less prone to accept the distortions and falsehoods that arise from our dealings with other peoples.

FRANK TANNENBAUM

3

All tongues and races are American,
All nations are embodied in her job,
To breed the noble concept of a man
Whose freedom is, that others should be free. . . .

RUSSELL W. DAVENPORT

WHAT IS

by Arthur Goodfriend

Simon and Schuster
New York

AMERICA?

FIRST PRINTING
LIBRARY OF CONGRESS CATALOG CARD NUMBER: 54–9795
MANUFACTURED IN THE UNITED STATES OF AMERICA
LITHOGRAPHED BY LIVERMORE AND KNIGHT COMPANY, PROVIDENCE, R. I.
BOUND BY H. WOLFF BOOK MFG. CO., INC., N.Y.

DEDICATION

The American Round Table forum was sponsored by the Advertising Council as a public service. Its purpose: "to develop a restatement, in modern terms, of the ideals, beliefs and dynamics of the American society."

In seven sessions, moderated by Paul G. Hoffman and Henry M. Wriston, forty-one distinguished specialists in American art, business, communications, education, letters, religion and science discussed these topics:

The Basic Elements of a Free Dynamic Society.

The Moral and Religious Basis of the American Society.

Our Concepts of Political and Civil Liberties.

An Examination of the American Economic System.

Cultural Aspects of the American Society.

It was at these sessions that the author, recently returned from a year's round-the-world mission for the Department of State, found an answer to the question people everywhere had asked him—"What is America?"

To the members of the American Round Table, for their wisdom, humility and honesty, he dedicates this book.

A. G.

The Tuscan Farmer knew exactly who he was. "My people have lived here since the world began. Sickness, hunger, the rule of strangers have we suffered. But we remain ourselves, true to the ways of our fathers. Like them, I am a farmer. Like them, I know my place. And who are you?"

"I am an American."

"And what is that?"

Others also wanted to know.

The man outside the mosque. "In what do Americans believe?"

The child in Athens. "Americans have shoes. I have none. Why?"

The woman of proud heritage. "We know about America's skyscrapers and assembly lines. But what of your blood, your code, your character?"

The hackman in France. "Tourists, students, businessmen—I ask them all. What *is* America? *Why* are you the people, the country you are?"

To these people who knew themselves so well, what was the answer?

Some Americans talked of Yankee ingenuity. Others quoted vaguely from the Bill of Rights. A few said simply, "It's something in the air." One or two confessed, "America? It is too big to explain!"

One man spoke of a group that, puzzled by the very questions the world was asking, sought the answers.

"They're looking beyond the stone and smoke. They're searching for the meaning of America. Why not listen?"

I listened for seven days while forty-one men and women sat around a table and talked about America. Who were they? What had brought them together? Why?

Geroid Robinson of Columbia University, it seemed, had posed a question. "Is it an idle dream that a group of qualified men might sit down together to distill and clarify the philosophy that is now embodied piecemeal in American life?"

A group of private citizens decided to find out what Robinson's suggestion might produce. To "The American Round Table," as they called it, they invited these men . . .

Frederick Lewis Allen (deceased). Formerly editor of *Harper's* Magazine and vice president of Harper and Brothers, publishers. An overseer of Harvard College and trustee of Bennington College. Author of *Only Yesterday, I Remember Distinctly* and *The Big Change.*

Ernest Angell, lawyer and member of the executive committee of the New York City Bar Association. Trustee of Briarcliff College. Chairman of the board of directors, American Civil Liberties Union. Author of *Supreme Court Primer.*

W. H. Auden, poet, playwright, author and anthologist. Neilsen Research Professor of English at Smith College. Editor of *Oxford Book of*

Light Verse and *Selections from Tennyson*. Author of *Another Time* and *Double Man*.

Chester I. Barnard, president of The Rockefeller Foundation and General Education Board. Formerly president of the New Jersey Bell Telephone Company. Director of National Bureau of Economic Research. Author of *The Functions of the Executive* and *Organization and Management*.

Elliot V. Bell, editor and publisher of *Business Week*. Chairman of the executive committee of the McGraw-Hill Publishing Company. Trustee of Vassar College and Lenox School. Vice chairman of the New York Power Authority. Member of the editorial board of *The New York Times*.

Eric Bentley, drama critic of *New Republic*.

Professor of English, Columbia Universit Formerly advisory editor, *The Kenyon Review* Author of *A Century of Hero Worship, The Play wright as Thinker* and *Bernard Shaw*. Editor of *From the Modern Repertoire*.

Denis Brogan, professor of political science a Cambridge University, England. Advisor to th British Broadcasting Corporation on curren American affairs. Author of *The American Poli ical System, Politics and Law in the Unite States* and *The American Character*.

Courtney C. Brown, Dean of the Graduat School of Business, Columbia University. A sistant to the chairman of the board of th Standard Oil Company of New Jersey. Formerl investment analyst and research director for th

14

ankers Trust Company and the Chase National
ank. Author of *Liquidity and Stability*.

John Ely Burchard, Dean, School of Human-
ies and Social Studies, Massachusetts Institute
Technology. Member of the Advisory Com-
ittees of the libraries of Princeton and Yale
niversities. A trustee of Mount Holyoke Col-
ge. Co-author of *The Evolving Home*.

Erwin D. Canham, editor of the *Christian
ience Monitor*. Past president of the American
ciety of Newspaper Editors. Member of the
ssociation of American Rhodes Scholars. A
litical analyst and news commentator.

Evans Clark, trustee of The Twentieth Cen-
ry Fund. Vice chairman of the Public Policy
mmittee of the Advertising Council. Member

of the American Economic Association, the
Council on Foreign Relations, the Academy of
Political Science. Author of *Financing the Consumer* and *Wartime Facts and Postwar Problems*.

Henry S. Commager, professor of history,
Columbia University. Author of *The American
Heritage* (with Allan Nevins), *America in Per-
spective, Majority Rule and Human Rights* and,
with others, *Civil Liberties Under Attack*.

Alistair Cooke, American correspondent for
the *Manchester Guardian*. Commentator on
American life for the British Broadcasting Cor-
poration. Author of *A Generation on Trial, One
Man's America, Christmas Eve* and *The Night
Watchmen*.

Russell W. Davenport (deceased). Formerly managing editor of *Fortune* Magazine, chief editorial writer for *Life* Magazine, and director of the experimental department of *Time* Magazine. Editor of *Life's* Round Tables. Author of *Through Traffic* and *My Country*.

Olin Downes, music critic for *The New York Times.* Lecturer on opera and on musical theory, history and appreciation at Boston University, Harvard University, the Brooklyn Academy of Arts and Sciences. Author of *The Lure of Music* and *Symphony Broadcasts*.

Peter F. Drucker, consultant on management organization to General Motors and the Chesapeake and Ohio Railroad. Author of *The End of Economic Man, The Concept of the Corporation* and *The New Society*.

Lewis Galantière, policy advisor to Radio Free Europe. Formerly a consultant on propaganda to the Department of State, director of French operations in the Office of War Information, and chief of foreign research for the Federal Reserve Bank of New York. Author of *America Today*.

Harry D. Gideonse, president of Brooklyn College. Member of the board of directors of the Woodrow Wilson Foundation. Chairman of the board of directors of Freedom House. Author of *America in a World Economy* and *The Higher Learning in a Democracy*.

Clinton S. Golden, labor consultant. Formerly vice chairman of the War Manpower Commission. Past officer of the United Steel Workers of America, the Brotherhood of Locomotive Firemen and Engineers and the Steelworker's Organization Committee. Author of *Soil and Steel* and, with Waring, *Dynamics of Industrial Democracy*.

Will Herberg, editor of *Judaism,* contributor to *The Jewish Frontier* and *Commentary,* and author of *Judaism and Modern Man*. Visiting lecturer on religion in universities and colleges in the United States and abroad.

Paul G. Hoffman, chairman of the board of the Studebaker Corporation. Formerly adminis-

trator of the Economic Cooperation Administration. Director of Encyclopaedia Britannica, Inc. and New York Life Insurance Company. Author of *Seven Roads to Safety* and *Peace Can Be Won*.

F. Ernest Johnson, secretary of the National Council of Churches of Christ. Emeritus professor of education at Columbia University. Chairman of the Committee on Religion and Education of the American Council on Education. Author of *The New Spirit in Industry* (with Holt) and *The Moral Base of the American Way of Life*.

Clyde K. M. Kluckhohn, director of the Russian Research Center and professor of anthropology at Harvard University. Director of the Institute of Ethnic Affairs. Associate Editor of *Comparative Psychology*. Past president of the American Anthropological Association. Author of *Personality in Nature, Society and Culture* (with Murray) and *Mirror for Man*.

Clara Savage Littledale, editor of *Parents* Magazine. Member of the National Committee on Parent Education, the U. S. Children's Bureau's Commission on Children and Youth, the Child Study Association of America, and the American Association of Adult Education.

Allan Nevins, professor of American history at Columbia University. Twice a Pulitzer prize winner in biography, and recipient of the Scribner Centenary and Bancroft prizes. Author of *The Emergence of Modern America, The United States in a Chaotic World* and, with Commager, *Heritage of America*.

James H. Nichols, associate professor of Christianity, University of Chicago Divinity School. Fellow of the National Council on Religion in Higher Education. Co-editor of *Journal of Religion*. Author of *Primer for Protestants* and *Democracy and the Churches*.

Norman Holmes Pearson, associate professor of English and director of the undergraduate program at Yale University. Member of the editorial board of the *American Quarterly*, and of the advisory board of *Perspectives, U.S.A.*

Editor of *The Complete Novels of Hawthorne*, *The Oxford Anthology of American Literature* (with W. R. Benét).

Daniel Catton Rich, director of the Art Institute of Chicago, and a writer on art. Formerly chairman of committees on painting and sculpture for the Tate Gallery, the American Institute of France, the Federal Art Project of Illinois.

Gilbert Seldes, writer, playwright, producer and commentator. Author of *This is America*, *The Movies Come From America*, *Lysistrata*, *The Years of the Locust*, *The Stammering Century* and *Wings of the Eagle*.

George N. Shuster, president of Hunter College. Chairman of the board of the Institute for International Education. Chairman of the Committee on Discrimination in the Nation's Capital. Author of *The Catholic Spirit in America*, *The Eternal Magnet*, *The Strong Man Rules* and *Religion and Education*.

Boris B. Shishkin, economist for the American Federation of Labor, and writer and radio commentator on labor problems. Vice president of the National Bureau of Economic Research. Member of the President's Committees on Civil Rights and Fair Employment Practices Act.

Edmund W. Sinnott, dean of the Graduate School, director of the Sheffield Scientific School, chairman of the Division of Science and Sterling Professor of Botany at Yale University. Past president of the American Association for the Advancement of Science. Author of *Cell and Psyche* and *Principles of Genetics*.

Frederick Martin Stern, business man, economist and commentator. Author of *The Junker Menace* and *Capitalism in America—a Classless Society*. Contributor to magazines.

Frank Tannenbaum, professor of Latin American history at Columbia University. Author of *The Labor Movement*, *Crime and Community*, *Slave and Citizen* and *A Philosophy of Labor*.

Francis H. Taylor, director of the Metropolitan Museum of Art in New York. Fellow of the American Academy of Arts and Sciences. Vice president of the American Association of Museums. Author of *The Taste of Angels*, and *A History of Art Collection from Rameses to Napoleon*.

Cameron Thomson, president of the Northwest Bancorporation and director of the Foundation for American Agriculture and McCormick Theological Seminary. Formerly president of the American Institute of Banking.

Jacob Viner, professor of economics at Princeton University. Fellow of the American Academy of Arts and Sciences and the American Philosophical Society. Author of *Dumping—A Problem in International Trade*, *Studies on the Theory of International Trade* and *Trade Relations Between Free Market and Controlled Economics*.

Walter H. Wheeler, Jr., businessman and president of Pitney-Bowes, Inc. Formerly a regional director of the War Production Board. A contributor to the *Public Relations Journal*.

Henry M. Wriston, president of Brown University, and trustee of the Carnegie Foundation for Advancement of Teaching, the Carnegie Foundation for International Peace and the World Peace Foundation. Past president of the Association of American Universities. Author of *Prepare for Peace*, *Challenge to Freedom* and *Executive Agents in American Foreign Relations*.

James Webb Young, senior consultant to J. Walter Thompson Company. Consultant on communications to the Mutual Security Administration and the Ford Foundation. Founder and past chairman of the Advertising Council. Author of *A Technique for Producing Ideas* and *Some Advertising Responsibilities in a Dynamic Society*.

Robert E. Wilson, chairman of the board of the Standard Oil Company of Indiana. Director of the Chase National Bank of New York, the First National Bank of Chicago and the American Petroleum Institute. Vice president of National Association of Manufacturers. Trustee of the College of Wooster and the University of Chicago.

Freely, these men talked about a nation of 160 million souls, about five hundred years of time, about the ideas and ideals and sweat and blood that had made America. Patiently, they probed its political, cultural, spiritual and economic wellsprings. Humbly, they faced its imperfections.

Somehow, in their words, I recognized familiar figures . . . of family, teachers, friends . . . and the forces which, from infancy, had formed me. Little by little, these men led me to a better understanding of myself. Knowing myself, I could see my country in clearer focus.

Listening, I wondered whether the American Round Table could become for others the deeply personal experience it was for me. Might its words, restated and tested in terms of one American's lifespan, guide others to the understanding which each must find for himself? The Greek child, the Tuscan farmer and others baffled by America's bigness and strangeness . . . might they perhaps grasp the meaning of one American's life?

I began to jot down some of the things they were saying at the Round Table. And as I wrote, I remembered. . . .

WHAT IS AMERICA?

Forty-five years ago, on the street where I was born, families from everywhere lived a wall's width apart.

I played with Nick, whose parents came from Italy. Hans, whose father was German. Phil, whose folks had fled a Russian pogrom. Jimmy Kee, the Chinese laundryman's boy. Bob, whose great-grandfather had come from Africa, a slave.

CANHAM: *Whatever we have been able to achieve has been the result of the inherent harmony of the inheritance which we have received from other cultures . . . not merely in what is called the West, but what is called the East as well.*

STERN: *In America it is a greater honor to be a self-made man than to be an heir, because we respect a man much more for his own achievements than for those of his ancestors.*

My parents came from Austria-Hungary. "It was a crossroads for armies from east and west," said my father. "In your veins might flow the blood of an Anglo-Saxon crusader, a Turk, a Roman legionnaire. You might even be a son of Genghis Kahn.

"Elsewhere it might matter. Here, you are an American. You are what you make of yourself. Nothing less. Nothing more."

COMMAGER: *American ingenuity has been fertilized and cross-fertilized by immigrants from all parts of the world.*

Nick's father fixed shoes. Hans's made wagons. Phil's father was a tailor. Jimmy's washed clothes. Bob's father took care of our houses. Mine made cigars.

In our street there also lived a French baker, an Armenian rug

dealer, a Czech butcher, a Syrian printer. It smelled of stuffed cabbage, dill pickles, incense and Havana tobacco. Like hundreds of other streets . . . in Chicago, Cleveland, Detroit, San Francisco . . . it hummed with songs and stories of all the world.

At home each family clung to its old ways. In the street, they mingled, each striving to speak a common tongue, serving the others with its special skill.

ALLEN: *Americans look upon change with less fear than most peoples.*

WRISTON: *We were a people who were always ready to go where we believed we would be happier. . . .*

Each family had its own reason for coming to our street. But the reasons were often the same. Nick's father, perhaps, voiced one of the most common.

"We were like animals. We had nothing. We were nothing. And there was no hope. So we took a chance and came."

HERBERG: *Freedom is rooted in the conviction that God alone is absolute Lord, and that no man is another's master.*

Phil's father told about the czar.

"He was the law. It is not right for a man to have such power. Does not the Talmud say, 'Unto Me are the children of Israel slaves, not slaves unto slaves'? A man should worship God, not a czar."

HERBERG: *Judeo-Christian religion is God-centered. Man is made in the image of God, he is the child of God, and the object of His redemptive concern.*

Each family, in its own language, thanked God for its daily bread. Each of us grew up in his father's faith. Each, in different ways, learned the same truths. Above all earthly things ruled God. We were all His children. Nick, Hans, Bob, Jimmy, Phil . . . each was equally precious in His eyes. In Hebrew or Latin or German or some other language the others couldn't understand, each learned to give to no man the homage due only to God.

BROGAN: *The American idea of religion is that religion is very much this-worldly; that it is less a philosophical picture, it is a view of your duty here and now . . . of good works . . . of service.*

Sometimes religion divided the boys in our street. We called each other names and quarreled. But, little by little, we forged our faiths into a way of getting along. We spoke our common code in the slang of the gutter. "Do unto others as you would have others do unto you" became "Let me give you a hand." "To do justly and to love mercy and to walk humbly with thy God" became "Play fair" and "Quit picking on a little guy" and "Get off your high horse."

NEVINS: *Behind the concept of equality is a belief in individualism born of historic forces that are peculiarly American—the conditions of colonization and frontier life on this continent.*

"Wild West" was our favorite game. Some of us dressed up in suits such as the American Indians used to wear. The rest of us stuck chicken feathers in our caps. Whenever our mothers were too strict, or the tenements hemmed us in, we escaped to "the wide open spaces" where men were men and no man was better than his neighbor. We, sons of Italians, Africans, Germans, Hungarians, Russians and Chinese, became cowboys and Indians, scouts, bronco-busters, pioneers.

TANNENBAUM: *We have no class structure, we don't even sense it, we don't know what it means. . . . The national hero is not a prince, not a king, not a rich man—but a cowboy.*

Buffalo Bill was our hero. He was living proof of how a man could meet nature's challenge, facing the unknown with his own strength and skill. Who his father was didn't matter. To us, he stood for something much more important . . . adventure, chivalry, resourcefulness, bravery and, above all, freedom.

One day the Czech family moved from our street. "Where did they go?" I asked my father.

"Out west," he said, "to Chicago—like Buffalo Bill."

BARNARD: *When I was a poor boy, I used to walk around among the finer homes and wonder how I could ever get the money to live that way. In that sense, I was envious, yes. But it never occurred to me to think that I ought to have the other fellow's money in order to do it. We were envious in the sense that we were inculcated with the ambition to attain that status for ourselves.*

All around us, the booming city teemed with signs of wealth. Hans used to watch the fine carriages roll down the street. One day he got an idea. He made a wagon of his own with an old crate and roller skates. "This will do for now," he said. "Later I'll ride in the finest carriage in town."

The rest of us wasted no time envying the rich, or Hans. We all made wagons of our own.

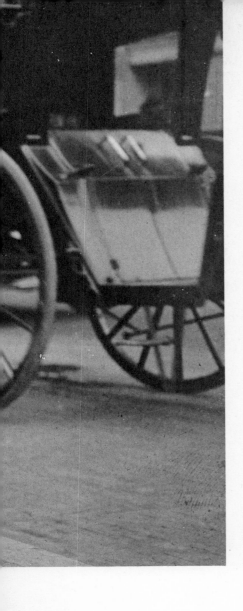

33

GALANTIERE: *We have limited the area of the so-called luxury goods. There are few things possessed by the rich which are not also the possession of the family of the worker. . . .*

One day my mother said she was tired of slaving over a stove. "For a few pennies I can buy food already cleaned and cooked, and save my strength for other things."

STERN: *American businessmen strive to make a mass commodity out of almost everything that used to be a class commodity.*

Most of the men in our street shaved every day.

"Why not?" asked my father. "Even I, a poor man, can afford the few cents it costs to buy soap and a good razor."

34

ALLEN: *We have something special . . . a culture which we do not think of as something for the elite, but as something which is accessible to practically everybody.*

Hans's family saved enough money to buy a talking machine. We spent rainy days listening to Caruso sing *Pagliacci*. It was the first time we ever heard opera. We liked it.

HOFFMAN: *If I had to sum up in one phrase the meaning of American society, I would say that it is a challenge to the individual.*

We read about a boy who sold magazines "to earn enough money to go to college." Poor kids go to college? Some of us scoffed.

But Bob said, "If other kids can work and go to college, so can I."

GALANTIERE: *The thing that is peculiar to America is the commonness of associations between people who have no other bond with their fellow citizens than their humanity, their citizenship and their concern for the good of the community.*

Most of the things that happened were so simple, no one noticed them. But my mother shook her head with wonder when everyone got together to clean the empty lots in our street. "No one forced us to do it. We ourselves decided the lots had to be cleaned. It is better when people do things themselves, instead of waiting for policemen and politicians to push them."

DAVENPORT: *This is unique in America; the development in private hands of social goals which elsewhere people have turned over to government.*

One day we went to the country for a picnic. "Who will pay for it?" my father asked.

The conductor explained. "The people decide something is needed. They get together. Everyone gives what he can—money or time or goods. Whether it's giving children happiness, or building a hospital, or protecting animals—we'd rather do it ourselves than depend on City Hall."

BELL: *In America, equality means simply that no handicap is imposed by society upon any child to prevent him from realizing the best that is in him.*

When we were six years old, we all were enrolled in the Public School. Jimmy Kee was scared. His mother took him by the hand. "You should be happy," she said, "and not afraid. In America every child has a chance to learn. It is the law. What happens when you grow up is up to you. Today, you go to school."

GALANTIERE: *It was intended by the founders that American polity should be founded in the belief that human rights or liberties come from God or from the nature of man, and that governments could not destroy those liberties.*

We learned to sing an American hymn.

"Our father, God, to thee, author of Liberty, to Thee we sing.
Long may our land be bright with freedom's holy light.
Protect us with Thy might, Great God, our King."

WRISTON: *The Declaration of Independence does start with one assertion which is so out of keeping with its immediate environment that it perhaps set a pattern for American thought. It is fundamentally egalitarian in a non-egalitarian world.*

We learned about the people who founded America. When the teacher asked, "Who were the Pilgrims?" Jimmy raised his hand. "My father is a Pilgrim," he said. "He came to America from somewhere else. He didn't want to be bossed around by a warlord or landlord. He wanted to live and work and pray in his own way. He risked his life to get what he wanted most—freedom."

We memorized the Declaration of Independence . . . "all men are created equal, . . . they are endowed by their Creator with certain unalienable Rights, . . . among these are Life, Liberty and the pursuit of Happiness."

NICHOLS: *The equality in the Declaration of Independence is an equality of opportunity and responsibility. These last are the gift of God for which he requires an accounting, and cannot be alienated to any body or constitution. This springs from the novel conviction . . . that private citizens were responsible before God for the character of state actions.*

When Nick heard about liberty, he stopped coming to school. Mr. Monahan, the policeman, asked him why. "It's a free country," said Nick. "I'm a free man. I can do whatever makes me happy."

Mr. Monahan said, "Nick, a slave can afford to be ignorant, but a free man must be smart. If he doesn't know how to run his own life wisely and obey the rules the people agree on for the common good —then someone will come along with a bigger club than mine. He'll make the rules and force you to obey."

Nick came back to school.

GIDEONSE: *The men who drafted the American Constitution did not assume the infinite perfectibility of man. Their whole concern about the dispersion of controls, about checks and balances, was based on a profound distrust of any man who acquired too much power.*

Our history books taught us to fear, above all things, the abuse of power.

1776 Tom Paine writes *Common Sense.* "A thirst for absolute power," he warns, "is the natural disease of monarchy." Americans resolve to cast aside one-man rule.

1779 Hamilton demands privileges for the rich "to check the unsteadiness of the poor." Jefferson fights against "the aristocracy of wealth" and wins.

1823 President James Monroe warns Europe's kings "not to attempt to extend their system to the western hemisphere." An ideal sweeps the continent . . . the right of men to rule themselves.

1861 Civil war tests whether a nation "conceived in liberty and dedicated to the proposition that all men are created equal can long endure." The nation endures, slavery ends.

1873 Giant corporations seek control of America's resources. Small businessmen, farmers, workers rally to fight monopoly and to free competition.

1779 America's new Constitution divides power among the President, Congress and Supreme Court. The Bill of Rights guarantees the people's freedoms.

1832 "When laws make the rich richer," writes President Andrew Jackson, "humble citizens have a right to complain." Their complaints break a bankers' monopoly on the nation's money.

1901 President "Teddy" Roosevelt declares war on "malefactors of great wealth," using anti-trust laws to "bust the trusts." In business as in government, Americans distrust concentrated power.

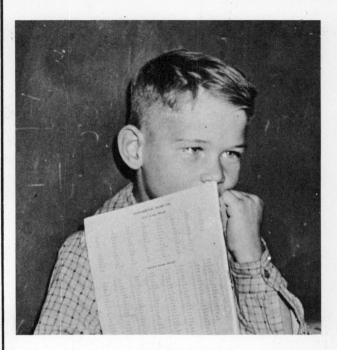

TANNENBAUM: *Our constitutional system has provided a vehicle for continuous revolution. . . . We can absorb very great shocks without seriously affecting either the stability or the inner sense of security of the nation.*

We wrote compositions on "What it means to be an American." Hans won first prize.

"In America, freedom has been tested by wars, bad times, slavery, trusts and strikes. Each time the people thrashed things out openly, decided what was right, and fixed things by changing old ways to meet new needs.

"To be an American means to trust the people, and to change laws peacefully to meet the nation's needs without changing the nation's main ideal—freedom."

COMMAGER: *A great number of societies have fundamentally the same moral and religious bases as we do. . . . The interesting thing is how it happened that we came out one place in this tradition and totalitarian states came out somewhere else. . . . It can be explained in the context of history, experience and actual practice, like practices on the playing fields, the ideals set forth in children's literature and inculcated in the young.*

Of all the great Americans we learned about, most of us loved these the best, as much for the little things they did as for the big.

George Washington cut down his father's favorite cherry tree and was brave enough to admit it. "Father," he said, "I cannot tell a lie."

Thomas Jefferson hitched his own horse outside the White House, to show that a president is no better than the people.

Ben Franklin came to Philadelphia, his pockets stuffed with buns. He worked hard, saved, and soon became a leading citizen.

Abraham Lincoln, born in a log cabin, studied by firelight. With nothing to help him but his brain and hands, he rose to president.

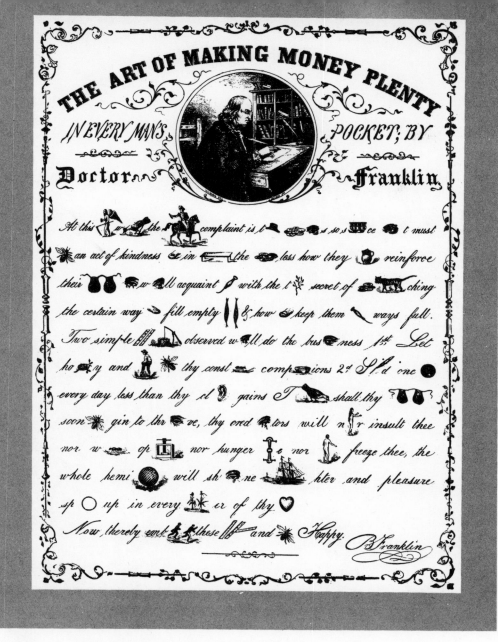

One of the first puzzles we worked out came from *Poor Richard's Almanack*, by Ben Franklin.

"At this time when the general complaint is that money is so scarce, it must be an act of kindness to inform the moneyless how they can reinforce their purses. I will acquaint all with the true secret of money catching, the certain way to fill empty purses and how to keep them always full. Two simple rules well observed will do the business. First, let honesty and labor be thy constant companions. Second, spend one coin every day less than thy clear gains. Then shall thy purses soon begin to thrive, thy creditors will never insult thee nor want oppress nor hunger bite nor nakedness freeze thee, the whole hemisphere will shine brighter and pleasure spring up in every corner of thy heart. Now thereby embrace these rules and be happy."

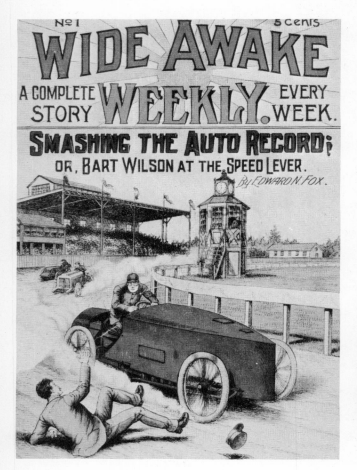

ALLEN: *Alger's paper-bound guides to success were and are generally regarded by educated readers as trash. . . . Yet they were the delight of millions of American boys . . . and it is possible that most of these boys got from Horatio Alger their first intelligible picture of American economic life.*

Outside school, the first books we read were about poor boys who earned their way to fortune and fame. Through honesty, perseverance and thrift, they overcame all hazards, and rose from rags to riches. *Bound to Rise, Sink or Swim, From Bootblack to Senator, Strive and Succeed* . . . we read them all. Tom Swift and Bart Wilson, marvels with machines, were also story-book heroes. We itched to build and operate autos, airplanes, radios like theirs.

VINER: *Most of the American people came here without status. They had a chance to get it here, but one of the conditions was that invariably they got it through income, and all the rewards were associated with income.*

"Work and save." History and fiction agreed that this simple formula ensured success. After school and weekends, we sold newspapers and magazines, shined shoes, ran errands, fixed things. Money, earned and saved in our own iron bank, could take us away from our street . . . to the "wild west," to college, to the better houses uptown where every family had a bathroom of its own.

My mother said, "In the old country, for a boy to work was the family's disgrace. Here, even rich children go out and earn money."

TANNENBAUM: *Our people have moved from lower to higher position in the social structure. . . . It is not unusual in the United States for an immigrant to be a member of the Senate, to be Mayor of New York City, Governor or a great industrialist.*

"Self-made men" . . . boys who had "lifted themselves by their bootstraps" . . . were not merely figures in fiction or part of the past. They were the flesh-and-blood heroes of our street.

Andrew Carnegie came from Scotland. Starting as a messenger boy, he built America's biggest steel mill. Now he was spending millions on public libraries.

Robert Wagner came from Germany. He sold newspapers, studied law nights, was elected to the Senate. All America was watching his fight for workers' rights.

Arturo Toscanini and Enrico Caruso came from Italy to win their way to fame and fortune by satisfying America's thirst for music. New inventions made their art available to millions.

Sam Gompers, an immigrant from England, headed my father's Cigar Makers' Union. Now he was organizing workers into a powerful Federation of Labor.

Booker T. Washington, born a slave, mined coal to earn an education. Famed as a writer and teacher, he was making Tuskegee a great Negro college.

Thomas Edison, of Scotch and Dutch blood, started as a newsboy, invented an electrical vote recorder. His inventions and fortune were both beyond count.

Al Smith, of Irish descent, once worked in a fish market. Democratic leader in the Senate, he was on his way to becoming four-time Governor of New York.

CANHAM: *In our country, leadership has to establish itself. It is not taken for granted. It is not the inherent right of any caste. It does not proceed from generation to generation. It must prove itself.*

If anyone ever came up from nowhere, it was a German-Irish boy called Babe Ruth. Born over a saloon, raised in a reform school for wayward boys, Babe was an "underdog," a steel-nerved competitor, a man who never knew when he was licked. When he started hitting home runs, Babe became our idol.

WHEELER: *Competition is not at all an idea of getting hold of what the other fellow has, beating him down, stepping on his neck, and climbing over him. It stems from the desire of the individual somehow to prove his own worth, his own potential.*

Somehow, baseball spelled America. To win, each player had to give the best that was in him . . . a sharp eye, fast feet, faster thinking. To win, each player had to fit in with eight others and play as part of a team. Teamwork was essential, but when the ball was pitched, it was up to the individual to hit it. To win was important, but not so important as playing fair. And if you lost, you shook hands with the winners and tried again. We played baseball every chance we had.

HOFFMAN: *We have found a genius for collective action that leaves the individual an individual. In fact, it enhances his status as an individual. At the same time it works for the common good.*

One day Nick said, "Each man playing for himself won't get us anywhere. Let's get together and form a team. We'll learn to play real baseball that way."

WHEELER: *We give credit to the leader who takes responsibility. We let him come right up . . . but we won't take any driving. He has got to lead.*

Bob was our best player. But he didn't boast about it, or boss us around. He showed us better ways to hit and field the ball. We elected him captain of our team.

HOFFMAN: *It is a deep-seated belief on the part of almost all Americans that their success will be better assured as they help to build the success of others.*

At first we lost. It was because of Phil. He struck out, sometimes with bases full. We coached him, taped his bat, pitched to him. His batting got better. We started to win.

GALANTIERE: *The fundamental fact which emerges is the elimination of class warfare in the United States. . . .*

Some of the boys we played were rich. They wore uniforms. But skill and teamwork, not uniforms, win ball games. We beat them, shook their hands, promised them another chance.

CANHAM: *American society is characterized by spontaneous, voluntary, non-governmental cooperation of citizens in their local communities. It is brotherhood in action.*

Later, we had uniforms too . . . and Louisville slugger bats, a coach, a clubroom, and showers after the game. It happened when we joined the Young Men's Christian Association. "Y's" and settlement houses were being built all over town, paid for by businessmen and others interested in kids. Religion or race or money didn't matter. Most of us belonged.

Some of us roamed the streets in gangs. Roughness, toughness and size counted more than sportsmanship. A few never changed, and grew up to be gangsters and racketeers. But with "Y" men and other grownups to guide us, most of us picked up the rules of decency and fair play.

DRUCKER: *The individual is the central, rarest, most precious capital resource of our society.*

We joined the Boy Scouts too. We took the Oath: "On my honor I will do my best to do my duty to God and my country, and to obey the Scout law; to help other people at all times; to keep myself physically strong, mentally awake, and morally straight." We promised to do a good turn daily.

Did we live up to the oath? Far from it. But it stuck in our consciences. At least, we knew when we were doing wrong.

"Who is behind the Boy Scouts?" my father, ever-suspicious, wanted to know. "The government? The army? The rich?"

The scoutmaster laughed. "Nobody but the people. To bring up boys to be decent men and good citizens is a job we don't trust to anyone else."

BROGAN: *If there is a crisis of American taste, it is an aspect of that most important quality of American life, the feeling of the new American man that he is as good as anybody. . . . The crisis is accentuated by the national need to create a general national culture for a people of such diverse origins.*

Phil's mother called us barbarians. "Nothing but baseball, Alger and tying knots. Why don't they practice piano? Why don't they read Tolstoy? Why always Irving Berlin and never Beethoven? Where is their culture?"

Our culture was mainly in the movies. In the darkness of the theater, young and old, rich and poor, Italian, Hungarian, Chinese, Russian and German were one. Together we discovered entertainment and escape at a price everyone could pay, at a level everyone could understand.

PEARSON: *The realization of a classless society has meant a shift in the cultural pattern. The necessity to maintain production has meant a dependence upon the market. But it is a market whose aesthetic responses are not those of an elite group.*

For five cents we watched Tom Mix rout evil in Wild West melodramas . . . cheered underdogs like Charlie Chaplin and Harold Lloyd . . . envied the muscles of Douglas Fairbanks . . . raced to victory in powerful automobiles with Wallace Reid.

We learned about the rewards of goodness, the punishment of crime, the attractiveness of a fine body, the magic of machines. We added new words to our common tongue, and formed common values and goals.

PEARSON: *If there is a possibility of degrading the traditional culture of the elite, there is the opposite and opening potentiality for the common man. It is the latter avenue which provides the true excitement to the American scene.*

Above all, movies excited our imaginations and whetted our appetites for stories about places and people beyond the borders of our street. Whenever the movies were based on books . . . *The Spoilers,* by Rex Beach, for example, or *The Four Horsemen of the Apocalypse,* by Ibañez . . . we raced to the public library a few blocks away. Built and stocked by Andrew Carnegie's millions, its shelves offered something the movies often lacked . . . truth, emotion, higher realms of human thought and experience where each of us could venture, alone.

NEVINS: *Slowly our literature began to reflect a more mature, social-minded nation; romanticism was pushed into the background by tougher-minded books.*

We read *The Jungle,* by Upton Sinclair . . . *The Shame of the Cities,* by Lincoln Steffens . . . *The Octopus,* by Frank Norris . . . *O Pioneers,* by Willa Cather. We discovered around us social injustice, poverty, corruption and crime we had never noticed before. We glimpsed monopoly's effort to capture the nation's wealth, indifferent to the plight of honest businessmen and workers.

"How can a public library spend Carnegie's money on books that tear down America?" Nick demanded.

"Thank God," said Bob, "otherwise how could America improve?"

WRISTON: *Those who are most deeply committed to the American system are most critical of it; they are filled with "a divine discontent."*

Every day, America was "torn down" by newspapers and magazines that, for a penny or two, everyone could afford. We read about politicians, enriching themselves at the people's expense . . . about violence and strikes, as workers fought against long hours and poor pay . . . about Negroes, accused of crimes, being beaten by mobs without a trial.

Every day America was "built up" by these same newspapers and magazines. They urged reforms to banish slums that fostered crime . . . encouraged citizens to oust corrupt officials . . . applauded crusaders who fought against evil in all its forms. Every day, newspapers exposed injustice, corruption, crime . . . and aroused public opinion against them.

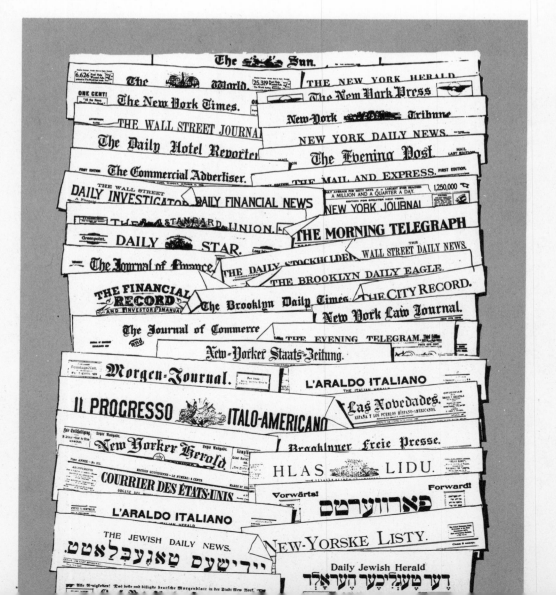

COMMAGER: *The fact is that censorship has always defeated its own purpose, for it creates in the end the kind of society that is incapable of exercising real discretion, incapable of doing an intelligent and honest job, and this guarantees a steady intellectual and cultural decline.*

Nothing was sacred to the newspapers. They attacked anyone they felt was wrong . . . be he president or some high official in the church. Some of us were puzzled by such "freedom of the press," but Hans's father smiled. "What do you want in the newspaper anyway?" he asked. "Praise for evildoers, or knocks on their knuckles every time they make mistakes? Newspapers make mistakes too, and sometimes go too far. But give me a country where papers are free to print the truth as they see it, and where people are free to buy whatever paper they please. In such a country, people can learn, think, act. In such a country, things improve."

GALANTIERE: *Is the goal to breed an elite or to breed a happy people? Up to now, all American efforts have been to breed a happy people.*

Above our classroom door stood the Statue of Liberty. The freedom it symbolized applied, in principle, to us all. None was to be singled out for special favor, by right of birth or wealth. Whatever life had to offer . . . a chance to dream dreams and plan their fulfillment . . . to vie with others on common terms . . . to taste the sweetness of self-earned victory . . . to achieve, with others, some common goal . . . to win, on merit alone, the respect and love of others . . . was to be offered equally to all. It didn't always work out that way, we discovered. But like Liberty's light, the goal shone bright and clear.

DAVENPORT: *We do not have a set of carefully worked out documents, all of which hang together logically. We have a mixed society which is part this and part that. . . . It would not be well to add this up into a doctrine . . . for the simple reason that you could not do it.*

At fourteen, most of us graduated from elementary school. An official from the Board of Education made a long speech about "the American system." We yawned, coughed, scratched. Already we had learned something about America the speaker didn't know, or had forgotten.

America didn't have a "system." America couldn't be explained in a speech. America could only be explained by little things that happened to people.

WRISTON: *We have worn the word "citizen" so smooth in our conversation that we forget "citizen" was a revolutionary word. It meant a man was a member of a community of equals, and that explains our attitude toward naturalization. If a foreigner came here and wanted to be one of us, he could join us as an equal. . . .*

America was the school our parents attended . . . where they learned English and American history and their duties and privileges as citizens of the United States. America was the day my father became a citizen. He swore an oath of allegiance and got his papers. But you didn't need to see the papers to know my father was a citizen. It shone in his eyes. "Mama," he said, "now I can vote. I have as much to say about running America as the richest man in the land."

WHEELER: *We seem constantly to be tearing ourselves asunder in debate and argue every question under the sun. But that very diversity is equality of opportunity for everybody to get up and express his opinion. Our strength lies in our equality and diversity.*

America was the first election in which my father voted . . . the political meetings in the street . . . . the candidates, hat in hand, taking the issues directly to the people . . . people arguing in little groups . . . then voting in secret.

"Before you'll even have a chance to vote," moaned my mother, "the country will be torn to pieces." My mother, for once, was wrong. America talked in many voices. But in the end, the people's voice was heard and heeded.

TANNENBAUM: *The things that have happened in America have happened because we don't make great plans. We make little plans. . . .*

America was the day my father quit his job and opened his own cigar store. "That's my personal Statue of Liberty," he said, pointing to the wooden Indian outside the door. "I'm my own boss. I'll make better cigars and sell them cheaper so even a poor man can smoke a good cigar."

Up and down the street, husbands and wives sat around kitchen tables and decided their own future. Some changed jobs. Some opened stores. Some moved west. Some stayed where they were.

WILSON: *Instead of hoarding it, it is the average American's habit to put by savings which are placed back into supplying industry's tools that have so amazingly multiplied the muscles of men.*

America was the day my aunt went to work for the telephone company. "For a nickel," she said, "people talk to someone miles away." My mother drew her savings and bought one share of the American Telephone Company.

"Telephones," she said, "have a big future. Now we own a part of the company, and will share the profits." "Stop dreaming," said my father, "we don't even own a telephone ourselves." "Now is the time," my mother said, "to save and sacrifice. Later *we'll* talk on a telephone too."

HOFFMAN: *I would put the presence of com petition and the presence of laws to enforc competition among the principal elements con tributing dynamism to our economy.*

America was the neighborhood grocery stor where my mother was queen, conferring h favor on this or that. America was shelves groan ing under goods, trying to catch the eye wit better quality at a lower price. America was th grocer, cleaning the floor, cutting prices, force to become a better businessman by the com petition of others determined to win my mother good will.

GALANTIERE: *In the matter of betterment of the masses . . . America has set the pace. America has found out how you do these things in the way of production and how you get them to the largest number of people at the cheapest price. . . .*

America was new ideas to tickle the imagination.

The sewing machine that saved my mother's eyesight.

My father's correspondence course in textile design.

The meccano set with which Bob engineered his first house.

The dream of our own piano.

America was the future . . . tempting, accessible, cheap.

CLARK: *The American economic system is far from perfect . . . its greatest defect is its striking instability; its proclivity to booms and depressions. . . .*

America was horses disappearing from the street. Wagon factories shutting down. Makers of harnesses losing their jobs. Breadlines, soup kitchens, slums around the corner from mansions and fine hotels.

America was the day Hans's father came home with his last pay check, cursing Henry Ford. America was the day my father closed his store, unable to compete with cheap mass-produced cigars and cigarettes.

DRUCKER: *What has happened in the United States has come about because . . . we accepted conflict and tried to utilize it, to turn it to account rather than suppress it into the harmony of the graveyard.*

America was the smell of gas, the roar of motors. Help-wanted signs outside automobile factories and garages. The day my father went to Paterson, New Jersey, to manufacture silk. The day Hans's father jubilantly came home with the news that Henry Ford was paying a minimum wage of $5 for an eight-hour day, instead of $2.40 for nine hours. America was an idea . . . that workers should be able to enjoy the product of their own labor, instead of such products going only to the rich.

NEVINS: *The Great War was fought with gusto, 364,000 casualties and a national altruism of rare purity.*

America was General Pershing marching down the avenue, bringing back victory but not an inch of added land, nor a human soul unwillingly under American domination.

GIDEONSE: *Fundamental to our country is the separation of controls . . . based upon a profound Calvinistic distrust of the concentration of power in any man's hands.*

America was Woodrow Wilson committing his country to the League of Nations . . . balked by a stubborn Congress angry because he had not first won the people's consent.

NEVINS: *Prohibition most dramatically revealed America's ever-restless, tireless experimentation, its inexhaustible will to try something new in the hope of something better.*

America was Andrew Volstead, the Anti-Saloon League, the Women's Christian Temperance Union. America was prohibition, speakeasies, bootleggers, bathtub gin.

COMMAGER: *If you pass a bad law you find out and correct it; some damage is done but not irreparable damage; the same group who passed the laws say, "Come, we made fools of ourselves and we will now repeal that law."*

America was a camel, symbol of thirst, marching down the avenue. America was people demanding repeal of prohibition, changing the Constitution to meet the people's will.

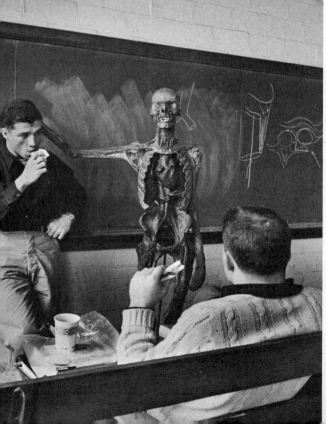

merica was all these things. But mostly America meant a chance to "get ahead." To each of us, getting ahead meant something different. To Hans, it meant machines. To Phil, a career in music. To Bob, architecture. To Jimmy, electrical engineering. To Nick, medicine. To me, a chance to write. To our parents, it meant a miracle . . . sons of immigrants and workers becoming doctors, artists, writers, engineers.

One day, after four years in high school, some of us found our names on the bulletin board . . . winners of scholarships to universities, or admitted to City College which, like high school, was free.

STERN: *We have in America developed the gold mine of talent in what Europeans call "the lower classes." Educational opportunities exist for all in this country. It is much easier in the United States for the son of a farmer or worker to have a high school education and even go to college and choose any job or profession for which he will qualify.*

COMMAGER: *The tradition of scholarship as a separate and rather exalted department of life has never taken a firm hold on American culture . . . art and scholarship are bogus unless they derive from life directly.*

We discovered the great books of the ages. "Don't hide behind them," said the professor. "Make their wisdom useful to your fellow men."

"Make wisdom useful" summed up the thought of America's greatest teachers, William James and John Dewey. Theirs was the functional approach . . . "pragmatism," they called it . . . to education for life. Not just to talk about things, but to learn to *do* them . . . to practice the arts and disciplines necessary in a scientific, industrial age . . . these ideas dominated and directed our college years.

AUDEN: *In a fluid society devoid of rigid class stratification, a distinction between courtly or academic art on the one side, and truly popular art on the other, is unlikely to persist. . . . There is today not enough difference in the way in which people live to make different types of art a reality in this society.*

In night-long "bull sessions," we discussed art, literature, philosophy. Whatever our specialties, the humanities interested us all. We disagreed on poets and painters, but Bob expressed one idea most of us shared.

"We're finished with the genteel tradition, with the authoritarian methods and outlook of the aristocrats. We want the clarity of Aristotle in a blueprint, the beauty of Da Vinci in a poster, the Iliad's grace in the daily paper. We want art not alone in museums, but in factories and dwellings, in pots and pans."

BARNARD: *The right to join what I want to join, to do what I want to do or to not do what I might do without giving anyone a reason —I believe that this right is responsible for a great deal of the dynamic effort of our country.*

College was more than books and bull-sessions. It was music, drama, debates . . . football, politics, religion. We joined with others equally dedicated to some common interest . . . formed orchestras and glee clubs, professional societies and teams. We learned to multiply our individual usefulness in free association with others who shared our aims.

Men also drew together into groups, based largely on social background, family, wealth. From some of these, Negroes, Catholics, Jews were barred. The right of a man to choose his friends was granted . . . but snobbery and racism became hot issues in our college publications and debates. To prove ourselves, to win esteem by excellence in our chosen field, was our answer to this social challenge.

STERN: *Our employers are forced to tap all resources of talent, intelligence, skill, wherever they find them, irrespective of class origin.*

Freedom of association was a freedom also enjoyed by employers. Bob and Jimmy fretted about their chances for a job. The corporation employment manager who interviewed Jimmy seemed unconcerned with the color of his skin, or that his grandfather raised rice in a paddy field near Canton. He studied Jimmy's record. He listened to him talk. He questioned Jimmy about his ideas on electronics. Then he asked, "When can you come to work?"

Negroes· had come a long way from slavery, but many doors remained shut. Bob shrugged. "I'm going west. I'll take any job and build up a little capital. Then I'll open an architect's office of my own."

CLARK: *The private business corporation is the dominant institution in American economic life. In its distinctively American form, it is probably more responsible for our economic performance than any other single feature. Without its limited liability feature, the large aggregations of capital which have revolutionized our economic life through mechanized mass production would have been impossible.*

Hans worked for an automobile corporation in Detroit. "On the assembly line," he wrote, "I help produce a thousand cars in the time my father made one wagon, and a lot better and cheaper. But it takes capital to build a factory like this."

Many of us invested our savings in corporation shares. Our money paid for Hans's tools and Jimmy's equipment. Without taking responsibility for the corporation's debts, we shared its profits. As purchasers of its products, or as workers, or as investors . . . or all three . . . we partook in the affairs of corporations. Teddy Roosevelt, Woodrow Wilson, the anti-trust laws had forged them into giant servants of all the people.

WRISTON: *Like all growths, American society is hospitable to parasites which may be bland, may be vicious, or may be beneficial. Often people mistake these for the reality.*

As business boomed, corporation shares rose in price. Little by little, we began to think less about machines and production, and more about paper stocks and profits. Even my mother, who once had read the Telephone Company's reports with a manager's eye, now read nothing but daily stock prices in the newspaper. Like millions of others, she borrowed money to buy more stock. We were no longer investors, but gamblers. When wheels of industry and trade slowed down around the world, stock prices toppled. Our dream of easy wealth blew up.

GALANTIERE: *Justice Holmes said, "There is nothing in the Constitution of the United States that prevents the American people from making damn fools of themselves."*

ALLEN: *The great depression marked millions of people inwardly for the rest of their lives. . . . Here were failure and defeat and want visiting the energetic along with the feckless, the able along with the unable, the virtuous along with the irresponsible. They found their fortunes interlocked with those of great numbers of other people in a pattern complex beyond their understanding.*

GIDEONSE: *The most brutal acts of the totalitarians are rooted in the naïve assumption that men can be entrusted with unlimited power—and that the outcome will be good. Our native instinct—and our religious tradition—has been otherwise.*

The crisis was bigger than our street and city. It gripped the nation and the world. Elsewhere, despairing people turned to dictators who pitted against poverty the greater evils of hatred and bloodshed. America, too, had its quota of demagogues and fools. But America, in the end, turned to the ballot box. Peacefully, we put a new president and congress into office. Quickly, laws were passed to feed the hungry, to bolster the banks, to create employment. Gradually, fear gave way to a new upsurge of confidence, tempered by awareness of the deep abyss so narrowly missed.

HERBERG: *Democracy's built-in principle of self-criticism and self-correction is the institutionalization of the continuing judgment of God upon man and all his works.*

In other lands, propagandists poured out praise of tyrants. In America, novels, plays, painting, publications ruthlessly exposed the plight of landless "Okies" . . . the agony of the bread-lines and shanty-towns . . . the Negro's bitter uphill fight. Nothing was hidden. Nothing was condoned. America, its conscience lashed, set out to correct social injustice that mocked the ideals of Washington, Jefferson, Lincoln.

GALANTIERE: *The outstanding characteristic of America is the refusal of Americans to accept defects in their society as irremediable.*

Within a decade, we saw the face of America change. Great dams turned dust bowls into gardens. New laws acknowledged the right of every man to security in sickness and old age. Speculation in stocks was regulated without hobbling the healthy willingness of men to risk their savings in new ventures. The battle against discrimination was waged against a stubborn foe.

Was America's way always wise? Was victory won? Not always. But the will was strong.

DRUCKER: *We have learned that productivity is a social if not a moral principle, and not just a business principle; that increased productivity must contribute to a greater income of the masses, to greater job security of the workers, to greater satisfaction of the consumer . . . and that it is not enough for it to contribute to profits.*

VINER: *Courtesy and respectful treatment of labor is now routine, is expected, and there is trouble if it doesn't come.*

From Hans came word of one of the deepest changes of all. "I sat down with management yesterday to thrash out problems in the shop. On the face of it, they represented the stockholders and I the workers. True, but it wasn't that simple, for many of the workers are stockholders too, and the managers are all salaried workers. We are all in the same boat and, thank God, at last we're beginning to admit it. We made headway on an adjustment of wages, based on living costs and a fair return for investors. With the power of the union behind it, labor's voice was heard."

As the boys from our street grew up, so did our tastes and values. Although we still accepted the movies' sensational hokum, we craved something better. From Hollywood, the radio, the group theater, the opera, came more mature fare. Phil, who played in a great philharmonic orchestra, tried to explain what had happened.

"For a while, in the depression, government sponsored the arts. We artists were grateful, but our very gratitude—our dependence on one sponsor—fed a fear that some day, someone would tell us what we must or must not play. We were glad when business corporations, private foundations and individuals took over. Control is now dispersed. Variety results. Commercialism, jingles, soap opera—they're the price to be paid for freedom to create and enjoy the good."

The good, perhaps, outweighed the bad. Lovers of dance joined to revive the ballet. Ballet mated with drama and opera, and plays like *Oklahoma!* were born. Drama itself flourished in a thousand schools and colleges. Every Sunday, America tuned in on Toscanini for unmarred hours of musical bliss; we bought millions of classical records. Individual Americans became patrons of the arts.

YOUNG: *Every human being has four hungers; the hunger of the loins, the hunger of the belly, the hunger of the mind, the hunger of the soul. You can get by a long time on the loins and the belly, but there is a good deal of evidence that even the meanest of men eventually crave something for the mind and soul.*

PEARSON: *It is the American conviction that direct governmental control of cultural activities is uncongenial to government, and tends to restrict the free expression of such interests and activities on the part of the people.*

GALANTIERE: *The great problem that we have in the United States is the problem that would face any society in which the greatest proportion of people had been given the purchasing power with which to satisfy whatever instincts they had for cultural objects. . . . In a free society, the market is solicited by all kinds of people—manufacturers, printers of comic books, Wheatsy-Teetsy producers, etc.*

DOWNES: *If the public is given a chance to discriminate, the tendency is always upward.*

BURCHARD: *The American dwelling house has been throughout our culture our greatest architectural distinction. . . . American buildings, in respect of the comforts they offer, convenience, general livability, are far ahead of buildings produced anywhere else in the world.*

In California, Bob's houses for workers—comfortable to live in, easy to keep clean—were winning wide acclaim. "Magazines, movies, radio programs," he wrote, "are teaching people to want modern houses. The resultant demand is so big, mass production savings cut costs to the bone. Builders, with union cooperation, are streamlining

construction techniques. Banks and government agencies are lending money at low interest. And so I can design a house for workers with advantages once enjoyed only by the rich. The slums are doomed. So is the notion that people must work in drab, uncomfortable factories, offices and shops."

PEARSON: *If one looks for recent monuments in America, there are Frank Lloyd Wright's buildings for the Johnson Wax Company, Saarinen's church, the concept of city planning in the design of Rockefeller Center; and in engineering, our dams and such bridges as the Bronx-Whitestone and the George Washington Bridge.*

WRISTON: *The government has been extraordinarily generous in financing rural electrification, in farm loans, in crop loans, in ceiling prices and in every way that you can imagine; in carrying out experimental stations, in developing transportation by road and so on. . . . There has been a relationship between government and the farmer which has increased productivity and yet has not created hostility.*

BROWN: *Voluntary organizations by and large are the instrument through which democratic society expresses itself.*

We all came to know a new America. We saw it in the tall wheat and the tall children of the farmers, protected against nature's whims by government price supports . . . in organized battles waged by citizens against heart disease, polio and cancer . . . in insurance policies and savings with which millions of individuals secured themselves against financial setbacks . . . in citizens' meetings, fraternal associations, businessmen's groups where civic improvement was the sole order of the day. We saw the blueprint of a new America come alive—aided where necessary by government—but based mainly on the people's will to run their own affairs.

HOFFMAN: *America is founded upon the idea of the right of the individual to own property . . . a right which is constantly under examination, a right which is being liberalized.*

Most of the boys from our street had long since married. "With a wife and kids," said Nick, "a man wants privacy, a door he can close, a few things that belong to his family."

Phil said, "When you start with faith in the dignity of man, you can't deliver yourself, like cattle, to the care of others. You take pride in taking care of yourself. You require the things you need to do it. To renounce one's right to own these things is to renounce belief in human personality. You can't do that and believe in God."

GIDEONSE: *In the last twenty-five years or so, the American conception of property has grown closer to the old Christian justification of property as an extension of human personality.*

STERN: *By education and occupation, Americans are completely unwarlike. In the last war, United States soldiers were known as the most homesick army in the world. Americans have too much to lose by war. And they know it, too; no demagogue can persuade them to the contrary.*

When war again engulfed the world, "Willie and Joe" spoke daily, in the soldiers' newspaper *Stars and Stripes*, the heartbreak and homesickness of the boys from our street. So did thousands of letters to the editor. I read them all, for I was the editor of *Stars and Stripes*. I searched for a clue to the paradox of their valor and sacrifice, their loathing and loneliness.

In a letter from an infantryman in a hospital near Metz, came a clue to the answer.

"Why do we fight? Because man is charged by God with responsibility for his own actions. He cannot forfeit this responsibility to a leader or to the State. Tyranny, dictatorship are the repudiation of this responsibility.

"We despise war. We will fight neither for land nor for wealth nor for glory. But when slavery threatens, when one man seeks power over others without their consent, when our basic belief in the sanctity of human personality is challenged, America fights."

WHEELER: *Individual man owes his first allegiance and responsibility only to God. We do not accept the notion that the State is higher than man.*

TAYLOR: *You can't send twelve million people abroad in two generations and not arouse their curiosity somewhat.*

PEARSON: *Self-consciousness in culture takes on a peculiar agony for Americans, since in a philosophy where all things are possible, the absence of complete success seems to spell failure.*

GALANTIERE: *I doubt if you can find in modern history an example of a people learning as fast from their mistakes as the American people have done since the 1920's. The change in attitude to a U.N. from that to a League of Nations; the difference between Lend-Lease and the inter-ally debt wrangles; the difference between the Truman Doctrine of 1947 and the rejection of a guarantee of the Franco-Prussian frontier in 1919—all this is part of a truly astonishing record.*

From Europe, Asia, Africa, we came back to our streets. We brought back memories of the villages our fathers had dared to leave. We knew that but for our fathers' courage and the grace of God, there were we, barefoot, hungry, hopeless. We brought back memories of Rome, Paris and Peking. We felt humble before the challenge of their beauty. We brought back fresh eyes to see the miracle of America, and consciences stirred by the world's misery, and minds educated to the swiftness of an airplane's flight and the narrowness of the seas that separated our wealth from others' poverty. Part of us we left with our dead: the pretense that America ever again could go its own way alone, unmindful of what we had to give to others, and of what others had to give to us.

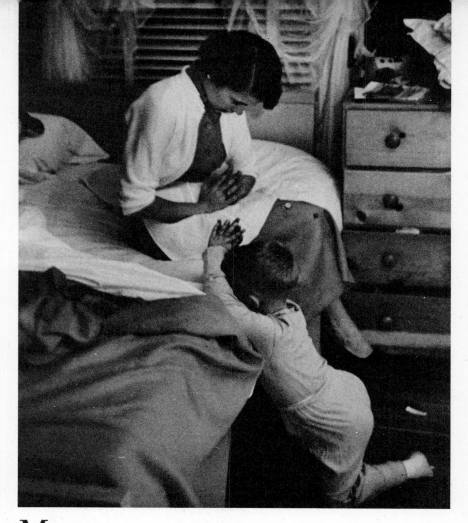

My wife is a woman of French and Spanish blood. We built our home in a village not far from where the Pilgrims came ashore. Here, in the cradle of America, our son was born. Here, in our village, he too is learning the meaning of America.

His is an America of trees and fields, of white steeples and hay-filled barns. But it is the same America, underneath, in which the boys in our street grew up. Here, too, people from all over the world live, if not a wall's width, a meadow's width apart. The names on their mail boxes sing of England, Sweden, Poland, Germany, France. Some families have lived here for two hundred years. Others are refugees from the Second World War.

Though the dates differ, their reasons for coming are the same. None would bow his head to a mortal master. All believed that they were equally entitled to life, liberty and the pursuit of happiness.

HERBERG: *The conviction that man is under the command of God I take to be the heart of the religious tradition of our society.*

DRUCKER: *The individual is responsible to live in Christian charity with his neighbor and with mankind . . . whatever happens in society is indeed his concern and sooner or later will come a day when a reckoning shall be demanded of him.*

ATKINSON: *Our culture represents a logical development from the independence, enterprise and willingness to work that characterized the pioneers who settled here two and three centuries ago.*

My son is learning to live and let live . . . to greet strangers as friends . . . to develop his brain and body and to exert them, in school and play, to the utmost . . . to compete with his fellows, eager for victory, but content with whatever his prowess fairly earns. Though he envied another boy's bicycle, he tried neither to

take it from him by force, nor from me as a gift. Somehow, my son preferred to mow lawns and mend fences, and earn the bicycle by himself. Having earned it, he takes good care of it. To own and care for personal property is a cherished local trait, visible in the clean houses and tidy gardens that line our village street.

VINER: *Accumulation, preservation and enlargement of your estate, taking good care of your children and their future, looking after your old age . . . all are part of the American cultural code, with religious support.*

COMMAGER: *The really urgent reason for allowing the widest latitude to the expression of the individual mind is that only the societies which encourage freedom of expression survive, flourish and prosper.*

Buffalo Bill has yielded to a cowboy called Hopalong Cassidy, but the legend of the frontier excites my son as once it did the boys in our street.

Alger's lessons of labor and thrift persist in the stories of living Americans that crowd his story-books and magazines.

Tom Swift and Bart Wilson long ago lost the race to Space Cadets and Superman, but the conquest of distance and time, the lure of machines, beckon brighter than before.

Chemicals, a magneto, an ancient Ford have joined the meccano; the urge to let science and industry lift the load from mankind's back is strong.

My son is seeking knowledge and truth in ways I never knew. But now, as then, no man may say, "This you *must* believe."

KLUCKHOHN: *The practice of democracy means that I, one person, one humble person, nevertheless feel some responsibility if the officials for whose election I was responsible go too far out of line.*

My son has attended his first town meeting, where the people of our village order the community's affairs. He has heard the man who tends the village dump oppose the opinion of the village millionaire, without rancor on either part. He has seen the people personally pass on how taxes will be raised and spent. He has watched the moderator count the vote, the calloused hand of a lumberjack as valid as the manicured hand of the local judge.

Here, better than I could in our street, he has seen the processes by which free men rule themselves. How the community's strength depends on the strength of each citizen . . . his industry, morality, responsibility and common sense.

WHEELER: *Our whole free dynamic society's future depends upon a continued growth of our sense of responsibility and morality in direct proportion to the increase in our material wealth.*

GALANTIERE: *Americans don't want government to come in and cure their ills. . . . Ours is a paradox of a society of individuals manifesting collective responsibility.*

The hospital where my son was born is supported, in part, by money raised in village fairs, organized by local businessmen. The hot lunches he eats in school are paid for and served by members of our Women's Club. The trout in our streams, the deer in our forests, are protected by our Fish and Game Club, which also supplies the scoutmaster and meeting room for the Boy Scout troop to which my son belongs.

In our village, people who boast of their individuality, and who consider ownership of property a sacred right, join freely with others to do the things that need doing. Things, they believe, better done by us, the people concerned, than by officials in the state capitol, twenty miles away.

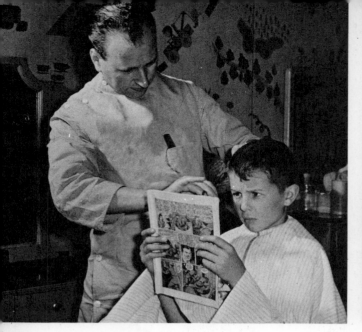

WRISTON: *We have a mass culture at a comparatively high level. But we are not unaware of the need for an elite, at least in the Jeffersonian sense of carrying every man to his highest potential.*

PEARSON: *The artist cannot despise the common man, since it is through the common man's capabilities that the uncommon man arises. . . . They are among the fortunate ones in a dynamic society who give height to a cultural base where all stand in common.*

Culture is a mixed matter in our village. Our children read comic books and practice piano. The repertoire of our dramatic club runs from *Silas Slick of Punkin Crick* to *Antigone*. Our paintings hang in

the village market. Our juke boxes play W. C. Handy; our home-spun orchestra, Aaron Copland. The aerials above our rooftops absorb many a tale of crime and marital misery, but we have seen and heard *Hamlet*, and *Amahl and the Night Visitors*, our first television opera. My son, who loves baseball, loves the Philharmonic too. He has heard and seen Lord Bertrand Russell, Robert Frost, Carl Sandburg, Frank Lloyd Wright. Not because these were faces and voices someone decreed he must see and hear, but because this was how he exercised his power of choice . . . the power in which lies the potential strength of America's culture.

TANNENBAUM: *We can't behave towards people as superiors or inferiors. . . . There isn't this feeling of status which defines permanently the relationship of one man to another.*

We have a commitment to live and let live . . . a commitment to the idea that another people has the same right as we to live its own life as we have to live ours. . . . Over no period of time have American people assumed the right to govern other people.

In our village, *Mayflower* descendants mix with recently arrived fugitives from communist terror. The woman who helps my wife with her housework is president of our Parent-Teacher Association. A lumberman, a plumber, a grocery clerk are our selectmen, elected to manage our village affairs. My son is learning to respect people, not for their blood lines and bank books, but for what they contribute to our village life.

Twice a day, my son passes the monument on the village green, to the men who died to abolish slavery, and to those who battled tyranny in two world wars. Nowhere in our village is there a monument to honor a man who seized land or wealth or dominion over others, by force of arms.

DAVENPORT: *It is not solutions that make ideas attractive. It is unsolved possibilities. The thing we all feel about America is that the possibilities are always unsolved.*

Recently I took my son to Washington. He looked at the dome of the capitol, shining in the sky. He looked at the street where we stood, a slum. "There's still a lot for us to do, isn't there?" said my son.

My son's eyes are open to America's faults as well as to its greatness. He knows evil when he sees it. He knows that there is plenty to be done. He knows that it is up to him to pitch in and help do it.

Here in our village, as everywhere, people are human and given both to virtue and sin. Here, as everywhere, perfection remains a distant goal, tantalizing, elusive, indistinct . . . a spur to thought and prayer and action . . . a daily reminder that man is required to take up the task of eliminating evil and to persevere, but that only God can complete.

Here, in our village, are happiness and hope, for our sons and daughters are free to think, and pray, and persevere.

TANNENBAUM: *We take nothing for granted; we accept nothing as perfect; we define nothing as the final end.*

From Nick, in Atlanta . . . from Bob, in San Francisco . . . from Hans, in Detroit . . . from Phil, in New York . . . from Jimmy, in Schenectady, come letters with tidings of new-born daughters and sons, of ambitions gained and withered dreams, of laughter and trouble and work and love. Through them all runs the same refrain. . . .

America is not a land of ease.
We have not paused from action to beget
Heroic smile and song and frieze;
We have no empire of the mind as yet,
Nor have we shed our light within the grave;
But as the sons of enterprise and sweat,
Honor the quick, the strong, the free, the brave,
The mind whose thoughts are cradled in the hand,
The fierce emancipator of the slave,
Exacting destiny of virgin land.
                    RUSSELL W. DAVENPORT

NEVINS: *Defying the pattern makers, (our Republic) is the hardest democracy in the world to get inside a book.*

What is America? Once, perhaps a Bryce, a Taine, a Tocqueville could answer. No daily cables, no films, no wireless and few tourists could disturb or dispute the image of America their books built in the minds of men.

But not today. Rare now is the Asian or African who has not seen an American salesman or soldier, technician or tourist. Rare is the child in Europe or Latin America who has not read an American comic or seen a Hollywood film. Rare is the farmer, however remote his paddy field or pampa, who has not glimpsed aloft an American plane.

Today, the task of explaining America rests with each American. Today, what others understand about America depends, in large part, on what each American understands about his heritage and himself. About the never-ending urge toward abundance for all . . . toward broader opportunity for each individual to develop his capacities to the fullest . . . toward a culture enriched by ceaseless self-criticism . . . toward higher and higher social goals, over strange thresholds. About America, ever young, ever bold, ever curious, ever eager for betterment and change.

Much that I had never known about my heritage . . . much that I had taken for granted about myself . . . I learned at the American Round Table. For the first time I saw myself as a product of America's ideals, beliefs and dynamics: As never before, I sensed my responsibility . . . to act, at home and abroad, in ways that did credit to those dynamics, ideals and beliefs.

America may indeed be hard to get inside a book. But America is inside all Americans. May each discover that part of himself that is America. May each pass on the best of it to his daughters and sons. May each, in all he thinks and says and does, carry America's true meaning to the Tuscan farmer, the Greek child, the man outside the Mosque.

A. G.

In writing this book, the author had the help of many people.

First, "the boys from our street" whose names are legion. Immigrants and sons of immigrants like David Sarnoff, Charles E. Wilson, Yehudi Menuhin, Adolph Zukor—who spoke for all when he wrote: "I do not believe my case was unique." Negroes like Ralph Bunche, Justice Hubert Delaney, Jackie Robinson, Paul Williams, winner of the Spingarn medal for his architectural achievement. Yankee neighbors named Cabot and Adams. Americans with names like Eisenhower, Lehman and La Guardia.

Second, the authorities quoted on these pages, whose wisdom and honesty evoked in the author a new awareness of the meaning of his own life . . . whose fuller meaning each reader must achieve for himself.

Third, the Advertising Council, a voluntary, non-profit organization of advertising and business men dedicated to public service, which broadened its mission—publicizing national needs like those for better schools, forest-fire prevention, student-nurse recruitment and U. S. Savings Bond purchases —to conceive and stage the American Round Table forums. From its head-quarters at 25 West 45th Street, New York, complete reports of Round Table sessions may be had.

Fourth, the publishers and photographers of *Life*, and Brown Brothers, the Bettmann Archive and Black Star . . . whose pictures of America, past and present, add warmth and color to his words.

And, finally, Frank C. Stockman, who arranged typography and design.

To all of these the author is grateful. To them belongs credit if these pages help others, at home and abroad, to understand America.

A. G.

Bradford, New Hampshire

What course a man will follow, or a nation, is set in no small measure by his basic creed, by what he really thinks about the true nature of the human being—his personality, his freedom, his destiny, his relation to others and to the rest of the universe. . . .

EDMUND W. SINNOTT

There can be no proper interpretation of yourself to others if you are confused about yourself. . . . The first job is to get some clarity of understanding about yourself, what you are, and where you are going.

HARRY D. GIDEONSE